Decentralized Finance (DeFi)

Unlocking The Future of Financial Freedom

BY

Michael McNaught

An educational book for readers of all ages.

Interested in learning about Decentralized Finance (DiFi)?

Well, this is the book for you!

Preface

-Poem

In the realm of DeFi, a digital frontier,

Where finance meets blockchain, innovation is clear.

Tokens are traded, contracts are smart,

A revolution is brewing, a brand new art.

Decentralized Finance, a world unbound,

Breaking away from the systems renowned.

No intermediaries, no central control,

A trustless system, empowering the soul.

Smart contracts govern, with precision and might,

Automating transactions, day and night.

Immutable records, transparent and fair,

Building a future that's beyond compare.

Lending and borrowing, without banks in sight,

Peer-to-peer interactions, a financial delight.

No lengthy processes, no endless wait,

Just instant access to your desired state.

Decentralized exchanges, where trades are made,
Tokens swapping hands, like a grand parade.
No need for intermediaries or middlemen,
Just peer-to-peer trading, time and again.

Yield farming and staking, a fruitful endeavor,
Earning rewards, like a financial treasure.
Locking up tokens, participating in pools,
Growing wealth in this world, breaking the rules.

Stablecoins offer stability, a harbor in the storm,
Cryptocurrency tied to an asset's norm.
Reducing volatility, bridging the gap,
A reliable store of value, avoiding mishap.

But in this realm, risks do exist,
Smart contract vulnerabilities persist.
Market volatility, scams and hacks,
Navigating the dangers requires strong facts.

Regulation and compliance, an ongoing debate,
Finding the balance, determining fate.
With governments and regulators in the mix,
Striking the right chord is a challenging fix.

Yet despite the challenges, the future looks bright,

DeFi's potential is a dazzling sight.

Financial inclusion, access for all,

Empowering individuals, standing tall.

In this digital age, where possibilities abound,

DeFi is revolutionizing finance, breaking new ground.

So let's explore this world, with open eyes,

Unleashing the power of DeFi, reaching the skies.

Hi there! My name is Michael McNaught, a scientist by profession, and an avid blockchain and digital currency enthusiast. I enjoy learning about this amazing cutting-edge technology and sharing my knowledge with others.

In recent years, a groundbreaking movement has been reshaping the world of finance. Decentralized Finance (DeFi) has emerged as a revolutionary paradigm that aims to transform traditional financial systems by leveraging blockchain technology and smart contracts. By eliminating intermediaries, reducing costs, and empowering individuals, DeFi opens up new possibilities for financial inclusion, innovation, and control over one's financial future.

This book is a comprehensive guide to understanding and navigating the world of DeFi. Whether you are a novice curious about decentralized finance or an experienced investor looking to dive deeper, this book provides the knowledge and insights needed to grasp the fundamental concepts, explore various DeFi applications, manage risks, and uncover investment opportunities.

Table of Contents

CHAPTER 1:

Understanding the Foundations of

Decentralized Finance

Section 1.1: What is Decentralized Finance?

Decentralized Finance, commonly known as DeFi, refers to a transformative movement that aims to revolutionize the traditional financial system by leveraging blockchain technology and smart contracts. DeFi encompasses a wide range of financial applications and services that operate on decentralized platforms, allowing individuals to engage in various financial activities without relying on intermediaries such as banks, brokers, or centralized institutions.

At its core, DeFi seeks to democratize finance by providing open and permissionless access to financial services, enabling individuals from all backgrounds to participate in global financial markets. By utilizing blockchain technology, DeFi applications aim to create a transparent, secure, and efficient ecosystem that promotes financial inclusion, innovation, and individual sovereignty over one's financial assets.

Section 1.2: The Advantages of Decentralization

Decentralization in finance offers numerous advantages that have the potential to transform the traditional financial landscape. Some key advantages of decentralized finance include:

1. Enhanced Accessibility: DeFi opens up financial services to a broader population by eliminating geographical barriers and providing access to anyone with an internet connection. This inclusivity empowers the unbanked and underbanked populations, who may have limited access to traditional financial institutions.

2. Financial Sovereignty: DeFi puts individuals in control of their financial assets and removes the need for third-party custodians. With decentralized applications and smart contracts, users can manage and transact with their assets directly, reducing dependence on intermediaries and providing greater autonomy.

3. Transparency and Auditability: The transparent nature of blockchain technology allows for real-time visibility and verification of transactions. All transactions and data are recorded on a public ledger, providing transparency and traceability. This transparency enhances trust and facilitates auditing processes.

4. Security and Resilience: DeFi applications utilize cryptographic protocols and smart contracts that provide robust security measures. By leveraging blockchain's decentralized nature, DeFi reduces the risk of single points of failure, making it more resistant to hacking, fraud, and censorship.

5. Efficiency and Cost Savings: Through automation and programmable smart contracts, DeFi eliminates manual processes, paperwork, and the need for intermediaries. This reduces operational costs, speeds up transaction settlements, and enhances overall efficiency in financial operations.

Section 1.3: Traditional Finance vs. Decentralized Finance

Traditional finance and decentralized finance represent two distinct models of financial systems with significant differences:

1.3.1. Intermediaries: Traditional finance relies heavily on intermediaries, such as banks, payment processors, and clearinghouses, to facilitate transactions and provide financial services. These intermediaries act as trusted third parties, adding layers of complexity, costs, and potential bottlenecks to the financial system. In contrast, DeFi aims to minimize or eliminate intermediaries, allowing for direct peer-to-peer transactions and disintermediation of financial services.

1.3.2. Control and Ownership: Traditional finance often involves relinquishing control and ownership of financial assets to intermediaries. In centralized systems, individuals must trust these intermediaries to manage and safeguard their assets. DeFi, on the other hand, provides users with full control and ownership of their assets through self-custody wallets and smart contracts. This reduces counterparty risk and enhances individual sovereignty over financial holdings.

1.3.3. Accessibility and Inclusion: Traditional finance systems may have barriers to entry, such as minimum balance requirements, credit checks, or geographic limitations. These barriers can exclude individuals who lack access to traditional banking services. DeFi, with its open and permissionless nature, aims to provide financial services to anyone with an internet connection, enabling global financial inclusion.

1.3.4. Innovation and Programmability: While traditional finance has undergone technological advancements, innovation is often constrained by legacy systems and regulatory frameworks. DeFi, built on blockchain technology, fosters innovation through open-source development, allowing anyone to build and improve upon existing protocols. The programmability of smart contracts enables the creation of sophisticated financial products and services, expanding the possibilities for innovation in the DeFi ecosystem.

In the subsequent chapters, we will delve deeper into the building blocks of DeFi, explore various DeFi applications, analyze the risks and challenges, and discuss investment strategies and the future of decentralized finance.

CHAPTER 2:

Building Blocks of DeFi

Section 2.1: Blockchain Technology and Smart Contracts

Blockchain technology serves as the foundation for decentralized finance (DeFi) applications. It is a distributed and immutable ledger that records transactions across multiple nodes in a network. The key features of blockchain technology that enable DeFi include:

1. Decentralization: Blockchain operates on a network of nodes, where each node maintains a copy of the ledger. This decentralized structure ensures that no single entity has control over the entire system, making it resistant to censorship and single points of failure.

2. Security: Transactions recorded on a blockchain are secured through cryptographic algorithms. The integrity of the data is ensured through consensus mechanisms such as proof of work (PoW), proof of stake (PoS), or other consensus algorithms, which require participants to validate and agree upon the state of the ledger.

3. Immutability: Once a transaction is recorded on the blockchain,

it becomes extremely difficult to alter or tamper with the data. This immutability enhances trust and provides a transparent and auditable history of transactions.

Smart contracts are self-executing contracts with the terms of the agreement directly written into code. They enable automated and trustless transactions without the need for intermediaries. Smart contracts operate on the blockchain and execute predefined actions when specific conditions are met. They play a crucial role in enabling decentralized applications and financial instruments within the DeFi ecosystem.

Section 2.2: Cryptocurrencies and Tokens

Cryptocurrencies serve as the native digital currencies within DeFi ecosystems. Bitcoin, the first and most well-known cryptocurrency, paved the way for the development of decentralized digital currencies. These cryptocurrencies operate on blockchain networks and enable peer-to-peer transactions with reduced reliance on traditional financial institutions.

Tokens, on the other hand, represent a broader category of digital assets that can have various functionalities within DeFi. Tokens can represent ownership in a project, provide access to specific services or products, or act as utility tokens within decentralized applications. Tokens are often created through initial coin offerings (ICOs) or token generation events (TGEs) and can be traded on decentralized exchanges (DEXs).

Section 2.3: Decentralized Applications (DApps)

Decentralized applications (DApps) are the software applications that leverage blockchain technology to provide decentralized services and solutions. DApps operate on a peer-to-peer network of computers or nodes, utilizing the principles of decentralization, transparency, and immutability.

DApps within the DeFi ecosystem enable various financial activities such as lending, borrowing, trading, asset management, and more. These applications utilize smart contracts to automate and enforce the terms and conditions of transactions, ensuring trust and security without the need for intermediaries.

Section 2.4: Oracles and Data Feeds

While blockchain technology provides security and immutability, it is unable to directly access real-world data. Oracles act as bridges between the blockchain and external data sources, providing smart contracts with off-chain information such as price feeds, market data, or real-world events.

Oracles play a crucial role in enabling DeFi applications to interact with real-world data and make informed decisions. They fetch data from trusted sources and deliver it to smart contracts, ensuring the accuracy and reliability of the information. Secure and decentralized oracles are essential for maintaining the integrity of DeFi applications and preventing manipulation or fraud.

In the subsequent chapters, we will delve into various DeFi applications, explore the risks and challenges associated with DeFi, discuss investment strategies, and examine the future of decentralized finance.

CHAPTER 3:

Exploring DeFi Applications

Section 3.1: Decentralized Exchanges (DEXs)

Decentralized exchanges (DEXs) are one of the most prominent and widely used DeFi applications. DEXs enable users to trade cryptocurrencies directly with each other without the need for intermediaries or centralized exchanges. They operate on blockchain networks and utilize smart contracts to facilitate peer-to-peer transactions.

DEXs offer several advantages over traditional centralized exchanges, including increased security, user control of funds, and reduced reliance on third-party custodians. Popular DEXs include Uniswap, SushiSwap, and PancakeSwap, which utilize automated market maker (AMM) models to provide liquidity and enable seamless token swapping.

Section 3.2: Decentralized Lending and Borrowing

Decentralized lending and borrowing platforms have emerged as key pillars of DeFi. These platforms enable individuals to lend their digital assets and earn interest or borrow assets by providing collateral. Smart contracts automate the lending and borrowing process, eliminating the need for intermediaries and enabling transparent and efficient transactions.

Decentralized lending protocols such as Compound, Aave, and MakerDAO have gained significant traction within the DeFi ecosystem. Users can lend their idle assets and earn interest, while borrowers can obtain loans by collateralizing their crypto assets, allowing for greater access to credit without relying on traditional financial institutions.

Section 3.3: Stablecoins and Algorithmic Stablecoins

Stablecoins play a crucial role in DeFi by providing stability and a bridge between the volatile cryptocurrency market and traditional financial systems. Stablecoins are digital assets designed to maintain a stable value, often pegged to a fiat currency such as the US Dollar or a basket of assets.

Traditional stablecoins, like Tether (USDT) and USD Coin (USDC), are backed by reserves held in bank accounts, providing stability through centralized custodianship. In contrast, algorithmic stablecoins, such as DAI and Terra, use complex algorithms and economic mechanisms to maintain price stability without relying on traditional reserves.

Section 3.4: Decentralized Insurance

Decentralized insurance platforms have emerged as a novel application within DeFi, providing coverage against risks and enabling users to protect their digital assets. These platforms operate on the principles of mutualization and peer-to-peer insurance, allowing users to pool funds and create decentralized insurance pools.

By leveraging smart contracts, decentralized insurance platforms automate the insurance process, ensuring transparent and efficient claims settlement. Users can insure their assets against risks such as smart contract vulnerabilities, exchange hacks, or other unforeseen events. Examples of decentralized insurance protocols include Nexus Mutual and Cover Protocol.

Section 3.5: Yield Farming and Liquidity Mining

Yield farming and liquidity mining have gained significant popularity within the DeFi space, offering users the opportunity to earn rewards for providing liquidity to decentralized platforms. Yield farming involves staking or lending assets in decentralized protocols to earn additional tokens or fees as rewards.

Liquidity mining, on the other hand, incentivizes users to provide liquidity to DEXs or other DeFi platforms. Users are rewarded with additional tokens as an incentive for contributing to the liquidity pool. These practices help bootstrap liquidity, incentivize participation, and foster the growth of DeFi ecosystems.

Section 3.6: Decentralized Asset Management

Decentralized asset management platforms enable users to manage and invest in digital assets through decentralized protocols and smart contracts. These platforms offer features such as portfolio management, automated trading strategies, and algorithmic asset allocation.

Decentralized asset management platforms provide individuals with greater control, transparency, and accessibility to financial instruments. Examples include Set Protocol, Melon, and Balancer, which allow users to create and manage decentralized index funds, token baskets, and automated strategies.

Section 3.7: Other DeFi Innovations

The DeFi ecosystem is a hotbed for innovation, and various other applications are emerging. These include prediction markets, decentralized identity solutions, decentralized derivatives trading, decentralized savings accounts, and more. Each of these applications aims to transform and disrupt traditional financial systems by leveraging the principles of decentralization and blockchain technology.

In the subsequent chapters, we will delve deeper into the risks and challenges associated with DeFi, discuss investment strategies within the DeFi space, and explore the future potential and advancements of decentralized finance.

CHAPTER 4:

Risks and Challenges in DeFi

Section 4.1: Smart Contract Vulnerabilities

Smart contracts, while revolutionary, are not immune to vulnerabilities. Coding errors or exploits in smart contracts can lead to significant financial losses or manipulation. Some common smart contract vulnerabilities include reentrancy attacks, front-running, and flash loan attacks. These vulnerabilities can be exploited by malicious actors to manipulate the outcome of transactions or siphon funds from DeFi protocols.

To mitigate these risks, thorough smart contract auditing, formal verification, and continuous monitoring are essential. Additionally, the development of best practices and standardized security frameworks can help enhance the security of smart contracts within the DeFi ecosystem.

Section 4.2: Price Volatility and Market Manipulation

The cryptocurrency market is known for its high price volatility, which poses risks to DeFi applications. Sudden price fluctuations can lead to collateral liquidations, affecting borrowers and lenders. Moreover, market manipulation, such as pump-and-dump schemes, can adversely impact the integrity and fairness of decentralized markets.

To address these risks, decentralized exchanges and lending platforms implement mechanisms such as decentralized price oracles, circuit breakers, and liquidity pools to mitigate the impact of extreme price movements. Robust risk management strategies, proper asset diversification, and continuous monitoring are crucial to navigating price volatility and preventing market manipulation.

Section 4.3: Regulatory and Legal Considerations

The regulatory landscape surrounding DeFi is still evolving, and navigating regulatory frameworks can be challenging. Various jurisdictions have different interpretations and approaches to decentralized finance, which can lead to uncertainty and potential legal risks. Compliance with know-your-customer (KYC) and anti-money laundering (AML) regulations can be particularly challenging within a decentralized ecosystem.

DeFi projects and participants should stay updated on regulatory developments and engage with regulatory authorities to ensure compliance. Collaboration between DeFi projects, legal experts, and regulatory bodies can help establish clear guidelines and regulatory frameworks that balance innovation and consumer protection.

Section 4.4: User Education and Security

DeFi puts the responsibility of asset management and security directly in the hands of users. However, many users may lack the necessary knowledge and understanding of the risks involved in using DeFi applications. Phishing attacks, impersonation scams, and improper handling of private keys are common security risks in DeFi.

User education and awareness initiatives are essential to promote responsible usage and secure practices within the DeFi ecosystem. Platforms and projects should prioritize user-friendly interfaces, provide clear instructions on security practices, and encourage the use of hardware wallets and multi-factor authentication to enhance user security.

Section 4.5: Scalability and Interoperability

As DeFi applications gain popularity, scalability and interoperability challenges arise. The current blockchain infrastructure faces scalability limitations, leading to high gas fees, network congestion, and slower transaction speeds. Interoperability between different blockchain networks and protocols is crucial to enable seamless communication and transfer of assets.

To address scalability and interoperability challenges, Layer 2 solutions, such as sidechains and state channels, are being developed to alleviate network congestion and reduce transaction costs. Additionally, projects focusing on cross-chain interoperability, like Polkadot and Cosmos, aim to enable communication and asset transfers between different blockchains.

In the subsequent chapters, we will discuss investment strategies within the DeFi space, explore the future potential and advancements of decentralized finance, and provide insights on how to navigate the risks and challenges associated with DeFi.

CHAPTER 5:

DeFi Investment Strategies and

Opportunities

Section 5.1: Evaluating DeFi Projects and Tokens

Investing in decentralized finance requires a thorough evaluation of projects and tokens to identify promising opportunities. Key factors to consider include the project's team, technology, community support, market demand, and underlying fundamentals. Conducting due diligence, reviewing whitepapers, assessing the project's roadmap, and analyzing its competitive landscape can help in making informed investment decisions.

Additionally, evaluating the token economics, such as token utility, distribution, and governance mechanisms, is crucial. Understanding how the token aligns with the project's goals and how it derives value is essential for assessing its potential for long-term success.

Section 5.2: Managing Risks in DeFi Investments

DeFi investments come with inherent risks, and managing these risks is crucial for maintaining a healthy portfolio. Risk management strategies include diversification, setting clear investment goals, and conducting thorough research before investing. It is also important to stay updated on market trends, regulatory developments, and security best practices.

Monitoring the overall health of DeFi projects, including auditing reports, security measures, and ongoing updates, can help identify potential risks. It is advisable to invest only what one can afford to lose and to be cautious of high-risk projects or unverified platforms.

Section 5.3: Diversification and Portfolio Management

Diversification is a fundamental strategy in DeFi investment to mitigate risks. Investing in a range of projects and tokens across different sectors can help balance potential gains and losses. Allocating investments to various categories, such as lending platforms, decentralized exchanges, or stablecoins, can provide exposure to different aspects of the DeFi ecosystem.

Active portfolio management is crucial in DeFi, as the market evolves rapidly. Regularly reviewing and rebalancing the portfolio based on market conditions and project performance is essential. This includes reassessing risk exposure, adding or reducing positions, and staying informed about new investment opportunities.

Section 5.4: DeFi Yield Strategies

Yield strategies play a significant role in DeFi investments, allowing investors to earn passive income on their holdings. Yield farming, liquidity mining, and staking are common strategies that involve providing liquidity or locking assets in DeFi protocols in exchange for rewards.

It is important to assess the risks associated with yield strategies, including impermanent loss, smart contract vulnerabilities, and potential token price volatility. Understanding the mechanics of the chosen strategy, evaluating the protocol's security measures, and monitoring the reward structure are key factors in successful yield generation.

Section 5.5: Long-term vs. Short-term Investment Perspectives

DeFi investments can be approached from both long-term and short-term perspectives. Long-term investors focus on projects with strong fundamentals, disruptive technology, and a sustainable roadmap. They aim to participate in the growth of the DeFi ecosystem over an extended period, understanding that market fluctuations may occur along the way.

Short-term investors, on the other hand, may take advantage of market volatility and short-term opportunities. They engage in trading strategies, such as arbitrage, swing trading, or taking advantage of token launches or events.

It is crucial to align investment strategies with individual risk tolerance, financial goals, and time horizons. A balanced approach that incorporates both long-term and short-term perspectives can help investors navigate the dynamic DeFi market effectively.

In the subsequent chapters, we will explore the future of decentralized finance, discuss emerging trends and innovations, and provide insights into the regulatory landscape and adoption of DeFi in traditional finance.

CHAPTER 6:

The Future of Decentralized Finance

Section 6.1: DeFi and the Democratization of Finance

Decentralized finance has the potential to democratize financial systems by providing open, accessible, and inclusive services to individuals globally. By removing intermediaries and reducing barriers to entry, DeFi empowers individuals to participate in financial activities, such as lending, borrowing, and investing, without relying on traditional financial institutions. This democratization of finance promotes financial inclusivity and allows individuals from all backgrounds to access previously unavailable opportunities.

Section 6.2: Integrating DeFi into Traditional Finance

As DeFi continues to evolve, the integration of decentralized finance into traditional financial systems becomes increasingly important. Collaboration between DeFi and traditional finance can bring benefits such as increased liquidity, efficient settlement processes, and improved access to capital. Partnerships between traditional financial institutions and DeFi platforms can bridge the gap between the two worlds and foster innovation in the financial sector.

Section 6.3: Scaling Solutions and Interoperability

Scalability remains a critical challenge for DeFi as it aims to accommodate a growing user base and handle increasing transaction volumes. Scaling solutions, such as Layer 2 protocols, sharding, and off-chain solutions, are being developed to address these scalability concerns. Additionally, interoperability between different blockchain networks and protocols is crucial for seamless communication and the transfer of assets across decentralized platforms. Advancements in scaling solutions and interoperability will contribute to the future growth and adoption of decentralized finance.

Section 6.4: Regulation and Compliance in DeFi

Regulatory considerations play a significant role in shaping the future of DeFi. As the DeFi ecosystem expands, regulatory frameworks are being developed to address concerns related to consumer protection, market integrity, and anti-money laundering measures. Balancing innovation and compliance is crucial for sustainable growth in the DeFi space. Collaboration between regulators, industry participants, and policymakers is essential to establish clear guidelines and regulations that foster innovation while ensuring a safe and secure environment for users.

Section 6.5: Social Impact and Financial Inclusion

Decentralized finance has the potential to drive significant social impact and improve financial inclusion. By providing access to financial services, such as savings, lending, and insurance, to underserved populations globally, DeFi can help bridge the gap between the unbanked and traditional financial systems. Moreover, DeFi applications can empower individuals in developing countries, enable cross-border transactions, and support entrepreneurship and economic growth.

In conclusion, the future of decentralized finance holds immense potential for transforming financial systems and empowering individuals worldwide. As DeFi continues to mature, its impact on democratizing finance, integrating with traditional systems, scalability, regulatory compliance, and social inclusion will shape the direction and adoption of decentralized finance in the years to come.

CHAPTER 7:

Popular DeFi dApps

Popular DeFi dApps:

1. Uniswap: Uniswap is a decentralized exchange (DEX) that allows users to trade ERC-20 tokens directly from their wallets. It gained significant popularity for its user-friendly interface and innovative automated market maker (AMM) model.

2. Aave: Aave is a decentralized lending and borrowing platform that enables users to lend and borrow various cryptocurrencies. It offers features like flash loans and allows users to earn interest on their deposits.

3. Compound: Compound is another lending and borrowing protocol that allows users to lend or borrow cryptocurrencies and earn interest or pay interest on their loans. It operates on an algorithmic interest rate model.

4. MakerDAO: MakerDAO is the creator of the DAI stablecoin, which is pegged to the US dollar. It is backed by collateral in the form of other cryptocurrencies and operates through a decentralized autonomous organization (DAO).

5. SushiSwap: SushiSwap is a decentralized exchange and AMM that gained popularity as a fork of Uniswap. It offers additional features like yield farming and token staking.

6. Curve Finance: Curve Finance is a decentralized exchange optimized for stablecoin trading. It focuses on low slippage and low fees for stablecoin swaps.

7. Yearn.finance: Yearn.finance is a DeFi protocol that automates yield farming strategies to optimize returns for users. It allows users to deposit funds into various yield farming strategies with the goal of maximizing yield.

It's advisable to do further research and check current trends and user adoption before making any investment or usage decisions.

CHAPTER 8:

DeFi Investment Tips

When it comes to investing in decentralized finance (DeFi), it's important to approach it with caution and conduct thorough research. Here are some tips to help you make informed investment decisions in the DeFi space:

1. Educate Yourself: Take the time to understand the fundamentals of decentralized finance, including blockchain technology, smart contracts, and the different types of DeFi applications available. This knowledge will help you make more informed investment decisions.

2. Conduct Due Diligence: Before investing in a DeFi project or token, conduct thorough due diligence. Research the project's team, technology, community support, roadmap, and underlying fundamentals. Review whitepapers, explore audits, and assess the project's competitive landscape.

3. Assess Token Economics: Understand the utility and value proposition of the token you're considering investing in. Evaluate how the token aligns with the project's goals, its distribution mechanisms, and governance structures. Look for tokens with

clear utility and a strong ecosystem.

4. Diversify Your Portfolio: Spread your investments across different DeFi projects and tokens to mitigate risks. Diversification can help balance potential gains and losses and protect your portfolio from the impact of a single project's failure.

5. Stay Updated on Security: DeFi platforms are not immune to security risks. Stay informed about the latest security best practices and be cautious about investing in platforms that have experienced security breaches in the past. Consider the security measures implemented by the projects you're interested in.

6. Monitor Market Trends: Keep an eye on market trends, news, and regulatory developments that may impact the DeFi ecosystem. Stay informed about any changes in regulations and compliance requirements to ensure you're investing in projects that align with legal frameworks.

7. Start with Small Investments: If you're new to DeFi investing, start with smaller investments until you become more familiar with the risks and dynamics of the ecosystem. It's important to invest only what you can afford to lose and to gradually increase your investment as you gain more experience and confidence.

8. Participate in DeFi Communities: Engage with the DeFi community, join relevant forums, and participate in discussions. Communities can provide valuable insights, updates, and tips on promising projects and investment opportunities.

9. Be Prepared for Volatility: DeFi markets can be highly volatile, and prices can fluctuate rapidly. Be prepared for price volatility and understand that short-term market movements don't always reflect the long-term potential of a project.

10. Seek Professional Advice: If you're unsure about any aspect of DeFi investing or need assistance, consider consulting with a financial advisor or professional who has experience in the cryptocurrency and blockchain space.

Remember, investing in DeFi carries risks, and it's important to make well-informed decisions based on your risk tolerance, financial goals, and market understanding.

CHAPTER 9:

Conclusion

In the book "Decentralized Finance (DeFi): Unlocking The Future Of Financial Freedom," we have delved into the exciting world of decentralized finance and explored its potential to revolutionize traditional financial systems. Throughout the chapters, we have gained a comprehensive understanding of DeFi's foundations, explored its building blocks, examined various applications, discussed the risks and challenges it faces, and explored investment strategies and opportunities. We have also contemplated the future of DeFi and its potential impact on society.

Decentralized finance, powered by blockchain technology and smart contracts, has emerged as a disruptive force that aims to democratize finance, remove intermediaries, and provide open and inclusive financial services to individuals across the globe. It has introduced a new paradigm where individuals can participate in lending, borrowing, trading, and other financial activities without relying on traditional financial institutions.

The advantages of decentralization in finance are evident. DeFi offers transparency, enhanced security, reduced costs, and increased accessibility. It allows individuals to have direct control over their funds, eliminates the need for intermediaries, and enables financial inclusion for the unbanked and underserved populations.

Throughout this book, we have explored the various facets of DeFi, including decentralized exchanges (DEXs), lending and borrowing platforms, stablecoins, insurance protocols, and innovative concepts like yield farming and decentralized asset management. We have also highlighted the risks and challenges that come with this nascent ecosystem, such as smart contract vulnerabilities, market volatility, regulatory considerations, and the importance of user education and security.

As we look towards the future of decentralized finance, it is clear that there is still much to be explored and developed. The integration of DeFi into traditional finance, scalability solutions, regulatory frameworks, and social impact considerations will shape the evolution of this ecosystem. Collaboration between regulators, industry participants, and policymakers is crucial to strike the right balance between innovation and compliance, ensuring a safe and secure environment for users.

Decentralized finance holds the potential to unlock financial freedom for individuals, reshape the financial landscape, and foster economic empowerment. It is a journey that requires ongoing research, learning, and adaptability. By embracing the opportunities presented by DeFi and staying informed about its developments, individuals can position themselves to benefit from this transformative movement.

Let us remember that DeFi is not a panacea, and caution is warranted in navigating this rapidly evolving landscape. However, with the right knowledge, careful consideration of risks, and an open mind, individuals can seize the opportunities presented by decentralized finance and play an active role in shaping the future of financial systems.

May this book serve as a guide to understanding the foundations, applications, risks, and opportunities within the world of decentralized finance, empowering readers to unlock the future of financial freedom.

Thank you for purchasing this book!

For additional reading on Blockchain Technology related topics, please check-out my other books (see below). Also, if you have enjoyed this book and have learned something new, please leave a book review rating on the site of purchase. Much appreciate!

1. Cryptocurrency Chronicles

   Unlocking The Secrets Of Blockchain Technology

2. A Deep Dive Into The Top 50 Cryptocurrencies

   A DYOR (Do Your Own Research) Guide

3. Common Crypto Investment Pitfalls and How To Avoid

   A DYOR (Do Your Own Research) Guide

4. The Digital Revolution

   Central Bank Digital Currencies (CBDC) Unveiled

5. Web 3.0

   Unleashing The Power Of Decentralized Connectivity

6. Artificial Intelligence (AI) Unleashed
   Exploring the Boundless Potential Of AI

www.ingramcontent.com/pod-product-compliance
Lightning Source LLC
Chambersburg PA
CBHW070844220526
45466CB00002B/883